W9-DIE-736

Knock-knock.
Who's there?
Evan.
Evan who?
Evan only knows!

Knock-knock.
Who's there?
Allison.
Allison who?
Allison Wonderland!

Knock-knock.
Who's there?
Ben and Anna.
Ben and Anna who?
Ben and Anna split!

By Dora Wood
Published by Ballantine Books:

500 WILD KNOCK-KNOCK JOKES FOR KIDS
500 WACKY KNOCK-KNOCK JOKES FOR KIDS
500 HILARIOUS KNOCK-KNOCK JOKES FOR KIDS
500 MORE WILD AND WACKY KNOCK-KNOCK
  JOKES FOR KIDS

500 WILD KNOCK-KNOCK JOKES FOR KIDS

Dora Wood

BALLANTINE BOOKS • NEW YORK

Copyright © 1993 by Dora Wood

All rights reserved under International and Pan-American Copyright Conventions. Published in the United States of America by Ballantine Books, a division of Random House, Inc., New York, and simultaneously in Canada by Random House of Canada Limited, Toronto.

http://www.randomhouse.com

Library of Congress Catalog Card Number: 92-97051

ISBN 0-345-38159-9

Printed in Canada

First Edition: March 1993

10 9 8 7 6

Contents

Introduction

Let's face it, knock-knock jokes are infectious and amusing. People always consider themselves clever when they "discover" one. In fact, they are!

I have gathered an amazing variety, and the challenge never diminishes. Almost anything can be the source of a knock-knock joke, as you probably know after reading my previous collection.

Would you like to share some of *your* knock-knock jokes with me? I would be happy to credit you if I include your joke in my third collection. You can write me at:

Dora Wood
P.O. Box 30373
New York, NY 10011-0104

I look forward to your creations. Thanks for sharing!

Some of my friends have already passed along many wonderful jokes and valuable suggestions. Michael M. Moore and Hector Leonardi have been particularly helpful. Many thanks.

Bjorn in the USA— Boys' Names

Knock-knock.
Who's there?
Aaron.
Aaron who?
Aaron'd boy!

Knock-knock.
Who's there?
Ahmed.
Ahmed who?
Ahmed my bed!

Knock-knock.
Who's there?
Alan.
Alan who?
Alan the family!

Knock-knock.
Who's there?
Allen.
Allen who?
Allen in a day's work.

Knock-knock.
Who's there?
Alf.
Alf who?
Alf way home!

Knock-knock.
Who's there?
Alfie.
Alfie who?
Alfie the cat while you're away.

Knock-knock.
Who's there?
Andy.
Andy who?
Andy man!

Knock-knock.
Who's there?
Bert.
Bert who?
Bert the steak.

Knock-knock.
Who's there?
Bjorn.
Bjorn who?
Bjorn in the USA!

Knock-knock.
Who's there?
Boris.
Boris who?
Boris the beef?

Knock-knock.
Who's there?
Brad.
Brad who?
Brad to meet ya!

Knock-knock.
Who's there?
Brandon.
Brandon who?
Brandon iron!

Knock-knock.
Who's there?
Brendan.
Brendan who?
Brendan break!

Knock-knock.
Who's there?
Brody.
Brody who?
Brody to the max!

Knock-knock.
Who's there?
Carlo.
Carlo who?
Carload of junk.

Knock-knock.
Who's there?
Cesar.
Cesar who?
Cesar before she gets away.

Knock-knock.
Who's there?
Chester.
Chester who?
Chester drawers.

Knock-knock.
Who's there?
Cole.
Cole who?
Cole as a cucumber!

Knock-knock.
Who's there?
Dale.
Dale who?
Dale come when you'll remember my name!

Knock-knock.
Who's there?
Danny.
Danny who?
Dannybody home?

Knock-knock.
Who's there?
Darren.
Darren who?
Darren the lead!

Knock-knock.
Who's there?
Derek.
Derek who?
Derek get richer and the poor get poorer!

Knock-knock.
Who's there?
Devlin.
Devlin who?
Devlin a blue dress!

Knock-knock.
Who's there?
Dewey.
Dewey who?
Dewey stay or do we go?

Knock-knock.
Who's there?
Diego.
Diego who?
Diego before the B!

Knock-knock.
Who's there?
Dion.
Dion who?
Dion my math test!

Knock-knock.
Who's there?
Duane.
Duane who?
Duane, Duane, go away!

Knock-knock.
Who's there?
Duane.
Duane who?
Duane the tub, I'm dwowning!

Knock-knock.
Who's there?
Dwight.
Dwight who?
Dwight wall tires!

Knock-knock.
Who's there?
Eddie.
Eddie who?
Eddie-body you want!

Knock-knock.
Who's there?
Edison.
Edison who?
Edison television!

Knock-knock.
Who's there?
Edward.
Edward who?
Edward really like to come out and play.

Knock-knock.
Who's there?
Eli.
Eli who?
Elies all the time!

Knock-knock.
Who's there?
Ellis.
Ellis who?
Ellis hot!

Knock-knock.
Who's there?
Ethan.
Ethan who?
Ethan lunch!

Knock-knock.
Who's there?
Evan.
Evan who?
Evan only knows!

Knock-knock.
Who's there?
Ezra.
Ezra who?
Ezra doctor in the house?

Knock-knock.
Who's there?
Felipe.
Felipe who?
Felipe glass with water, I'm thirsty!

Knock-knock.
Who's there?
Fletcher.
Fletcher who?
Fletcher the stick!

Knock-knock.
Who's there?
Francis.
Francis who?
Francis for lovers!

Knock-knock.
Who's there?
Frank.
Frank who?
Frank you very much!

Knock-knock.
Who's there?
Frederick.
Frederick who?
Frederick Express!

Knock-knock.
Who's there?
Gary.
Gary who?
Gary on!

Knock-knock.
Who's there?
Gidon.
Gidon who?
Gidon the horse.

Knock-knock.
Who's there?
Gil.
Gil who?
Gil the umpire!

Knock-knock.
Who's there?
Hayden.
Hayden who?
Hayden my homework!

Knock-knock.
Who's there?
Hank.
Hank who?
Hanks for the memories!

Knock-knock.
Who's there?
Howard.
Howard who?
Howard you know, even if I answered?

Knock-knock.
Who's there?
Howie.
Howie who?
Howie you?

Knock-knock.
Who's there?
Hugh.
Hugh who?
Hugh have to respond to my knock-knock jokes!

Knock-knock.
Who's there?
Hy.
Hy who?
Hy can't help it!

Knock-knock.
Who's there?
Ian.
Ian who?
Ian out of consciousness.

Knock-knock.
Who's there?
Isaac.
Isaac who?
Isaac my dog on you!

Knock-knock.
Who's there?
Ivan.
Ivan who?
Ivan awful headache!

Knock-knock.
Who's there?
Ivan.
Ivan who?
Ivan all the way so I wouldn't miss you.

Knock-knock.
Who's there?
Izzie.
Izzie who?
Izzie right or is he wrong?

Knock-knock.
Who's there?
Jack.
Jack who?
Jack pot.

Knock-knock.
Who's there?
Jacques.
Jacques who?
Jacques strap!

Knock-knock.
Who's there?
Jason.
Jason who?
Jason a fly ball!

Knock-knock.
Who's there?
Jeff.
Jeff who?
Jeff and see if your doorbell is working!

Knock-knock.
Who's there?
Jeffrey.
Jeffrey who?
Jeffrey good boy does fine!

Knock-knock.
Who's there?
Jerry.
Jerry who?
Jerry pie!

Knock-knock.
Who's there?
Jess.
Jess who?
Jess me and my shadow.

Knock-knock.
Who's there?
Jesse.
Jesse who?
Jesse if you recognize me!

Knock-knock.
Who's there?
Jethro.
Jethro who?
Jethro the ball, you're holding up the game!

Knock-knock.
Who's there?
Jim.
Jim who?
Jimbabwe.

Knock-knock.
Who's there?
Jimmy.
Jimmy who?
Jimmy a little kiss, will ya, hon?

Knock-knock.
Who's there?
Joe.
Joe who?
Joe out and play.

Knock-knock.
Who's there?
Jonah.
Jonah who?
Jonah Arc!

Knock-knock.
Who's there?
Jude.
Jude who?
Jude out!

Knock-knock.
Who's there?
Justin.
Justin who?
Justin the nick of time!

Knock-knock.
Who's there?
Kareem.
Kareem who?
Kareem of mushroom soup!

Knock-knock.
Who's there?
Keith.
Keith who?
Keith your hands to yourself!

Knock-knock.
Who's there?
Ken.
Ken who?
Ken you come out and play?

Knock-knock.
Who's there?
Kent.
Kent who?
Kent see you without my glasses.

Knock-knock.
Who's there?
Kesar.
Kesar who?
Kesar in the car!

Knock-knock.
Who's there?
Kevin.
Kevin who?
Kevin it all you got!

Knock-knock.
Who's there?
Knox.
Knox who?
Knox on wood!

Knock-knock.
Who's there?
Kogo.
Kogo who?
Kogo stick.

Knock-knock.
Who's there?
Kurt.
Kurt who?
Kurts and whey!

Knock-knock.
Who's there?
Kyle.
Kyle who?
Kyle be back!

Knock-knock.
Who's there?
Landon.
Landon who?
Landon the middle of trouble!

Knock-knock.
Who's there?
Leon.
Leon who?
Leonly way to fly!

Knock-knock.
Who's there?
Lon.
Lon who?
Lon, long ago!

Knock-knock.
Who's there?
Luke.
Luke who?
Luke out!

Knock-knock.
Who's there?
Luke.
Luke who?
Luke warm.

Knock-knock.
Who's there?
Malcolm.
Malcolm who?
Malcolm powder.

Knock-knock.
Who's there?
Matthew.
Matthew who?
Matthew is too tight.

Knock-knock.
Who's there?
Milt.
Milt who?
Milt the cow.

Knock-knock.
Who's there?
Norman.
Norman who?
Norman can make me happy.

Knock-knock.
Who's there?
Orrin.
Orrin who?
Orrin juice.

Knock-knock.
Who's there?
Orson.
Orson who?
Orson bucco.

Knock-knock.
Who's there?
Paul.
Paul who?
Paul up stakes!

Knock-knock.
Who's there?
Petie.
Petie who?
Petie Q Bach.

Knock-knock.
Who's there?
Pierre.
Pierre who?
Pierre the air.

Knock-knock.
Who's there?
Ray.
Ray who?
Ray drops keep falling on my head!

Knock-knock.
Who's there?
Russell.
Russell who?
Russell up some dinner, please.

Knock-knock.
Who's there?
Sid.
Sid who?
Sid down, you're rocking the boat.

Knock-knock.
Who's there?
Sonny.
Sonny who?
Sonny, Monday, and always!

Knock-knock.
Who's there?
Troy.
Troy who?
Troy and Troy again!

Knock-knock.
Who's there?
Tyrone.
Tyrone who?
Tyrone shoes, you're not a baby anymore.

Knock-knock.
Who's there?
Walter.
Walter who?
Walter wall carpeting!

Knock-knock.
Who's there?
Ward.
Ward who?
Wards and music!

Allison Wonderland— Girls' Names

Knock-knock.
Who's there?
Ada.
Ada who?
Ada the whole thing!

Knock-knock.
Who's there?
Ailene.
Ailene who?
Ailene against the wall!

Knock-knock.
Who's there?
Alani.
Alani who?
Alani have eyes for you!

Knock-knock.
Who's there?
Alba.
Alba who?
Alba seeing you.

Knock-knock.
Who's there?
Aleta.
Aleta who?
Aleta lunch now!

Knock-knock.
Who's there?
Ali.
Ali who?
Ali cat!

Knock-knock.
Who's there?
Allison.
Allison who?
Allison Wonderland!

Knock-knock.
Who's there?
Alma.
Alma who?
Alma love is for you!

Knock-knock.
Who's there?
Alma.
Alma who?
Alma mater.

Knock-knock.
Who's there?
Amanda.
Amanda who?
Amanda-lin!

Knock-knock.
Who's there?
Amanda.
Amanda who?
Amanda high fee.

Knock-knock.
Who's there?
Amber.
Amber who?
Amber-gur with fries!

Knock-knock.
Who's there?
Ahna.
Ahna who?
Ahna high horse!

Knock-knock.
Who's there?
Ann.
Ann who?
Ann eye for an eye!

Knock-knock.
Who's there?
Annie.
Annie who?
Annie-body home?

Knock-knock.
Who's there?
Anya.
Anya who?
Anya marks, get set, go!

Knock-knock.
Who's there?
Athena.
Athena who?
Athena many interesting things in my time.

Knock-knock.
Who's there?
Barbie.
Barbie who?
Barbie Q!

Knock-knock.
Who's there?
Bea.
Bea who?
Bea clown, be a clown!

Knock-knock.
Who's there?
Belle.
Belle who?
Belle-y dancer!

Knock-knock.
Who's there?
Bernadette.
Bernadette who?
Bernadette the stake!

Knock-knock.
Who's there?
Beth.
Beth who?
Beth wishes.

Knock-knock.
Who's there?
Bethany.
Bethany who?
Bethany good movies lately?

Knock-knock.
Who's there?
Bette.
Bette who?
Bette of nails!

Knock-knock.
Who's there?
Bianca.
Bianca who?
Bianca blue horizon!

Knock-knock.
Who's there?
Bridget.
Bridget who?
Bridget over troubled water!

Knock-knock.
Who's there?
Caitlin.
Caitlin who?
Caitlin you any more money!

Knock-knock.
Who's there?
Candace.
Candace who?
Candace be the last knock-knock joke?

Knock-knock.
Who's there?
Carlotta.
Carlotta who?
Carlotta mosquitoes out here!

Knock-knock.
Who's there?
Carmen.
Carmen who?
Carmen take a load off your feet!

Knock-knock.
Who's there?
Carrie.
Carrie who?
Carrie coals to Newcastle!

Knock-knock.
Who's there?
Carrie.
Carrie who?
Carrie my package, please.

Knock-knock.
Who's there?
Cathy.
Cathy who?
Cathy the brass ring!

Knock-knock.
Who's there?
Catlin.
Catlin who?
Catlin mouse!

Knock-knock.
Who's there?
Celeste.
Celeste who?
Celeste time I knock on your door!

Knock-knock.
Who's there?
Chloe.
Chloe who?
Chloe but no cigar!

Knock-knock.
Who's there?
Colleen.
Colleen who?
Colleen as a whistle!

Knock-knock.
Who's there?
Concha.
Concha who?
Concha recognize me?

Knock-knock.
Who's there?
Corrine.
Corrine who?
Corrine out of control!

Knock-knock.
Who's there?
Dakota.
Dakota who?
Dakota has been broken.

Knock-knock.
Who's there?
Danielle.
Danielle who?
Danielle so loud, I'm not deaf!

Knock-knock.
Who's there?
Dawn.
Dawn who?
Dawn to the wire!

Knock-knock.
Who's there?
Delta.
Delta who?
Delta bad hand, too bad.

Knock-knock.
Who's there?
Diana.
Diana who?
Diana to meet you!

Knock-knock.
Who's there?
Deb.
Deb who?
Deb as a doornail!

Knock-knock.
Who's there?
Donna.
Donna who?
Donna ask!

Knock-knock.
Who's there?
Edda.
Edda who?
Edda the class!

Knock-knock.
Who's there?
Edna.
Edna who?
Edna for a fall!

Knock-knock.
Who's there?
Ella.
Ella who?
Ella'va time!

Knock-knock.
Who's there?
Elsie.
Elsie who?
Elsie you in the funny papers!

Knock-knock.
Who's there?
Emma.
Emma who?
Emma makin' sense?

Knock-knock.
Who's there?
Emily.
Emily who?
Emily feud!

Knock-knock.
Who's there?
Enid.
Enid who?
Enid a new pair of jeans.

Knock-knock.
Who's there?
Erika.
Erika who?
Erika'd the car!

Knock-knock.
Who's there?
Erin.
Erin who?
Erin the tires!

Knock-knock.
Who's there?
Eureka.
Eureka who?
Eureka gasoline.

Knock-knock.
Who's there?
Eva.
Eva who?
Eva ho!

Knock-knock.
Who's there?
Eva.
Eva who?
Eva play the piano before?

Knock-knock.
Who's there?
Eve.
Eve who?
Evesdrop!

41

Knock-knock.
Who's there?
Fanny.
Fanny who?
Fanny you should ask!

Knock-knock.
Who's there?
Faye.
Faye who?
Faye'd away!

Knock-knock.
Who's there?
Flora.
Flora who?
Flora the Senate!

Knock-knock.
Who's there?
Gilda.
Gilda who?
Gilda the lily!

Knock-knock.
Who's there?
Ginny.
Ginny who?
Ginny pig's eye!

Knock-knock.
Who's there?
Gita.
Gita who?
Gita job!

Knock-knock.
Who's there?
Gladys.
Gladys who?
Gladys week is over.

Knock-knock.
Who's there?
Golda.
Golda who?
Golda man of the sea!

Knock-knock.
Who's there?
Greta.
Greta who?
Greta life!

Knock-knock.
Who's there?
Hannah.
Hannah who?
Hannah over fist!

Knock-knock.
Who's there?
Heather.
Heather who?
Heather report at six o'clock!

Knock-knock.
Who's there?
Hedda.
Hedda who?
Hedda for home!

Knock-knock.
Who's there?
Heidi.
Heidi who?
Heidi go seek!

Knock-knock.
Who's there?
Hester.
Hester who?
Hester a doctor in the house?

Knock-knock.
Who's there?
Ida.
Ida who?
Ida know!

Knock-knock.
Who's there?
Ima.
Ima who?
Ima in love with you!

Knock-knock.
Who's there?
Ines.
Ines who?
Ines on the prize!

Knock-knock.
Who's there?
Ingram.
Ingram who?
Ingram toe nail.

Knock-knock.
Who's there?
Ita.
Ita who?
Ita crow!

Knock-knock.
Who's there?
Jackie.
Jackie who?
Jackie in the box.

Knock-knock.
Who's there?
Jacqueline.
Jacqueline who?
Jacqueline Hyde!

Knock-knock.
Who's there?
Jael.
Jael who?
Jael University!

Knock-knock.
Who's there?
Jenny.
Jenny who?
Jenny chance you'd go out with me?

Knock-knock.
Who's there?
Jess.
Jess who?
Jess open the door!

Knock-knock.
Who's there?
Juana.
Juana who?
Juana big kiss?

Knock-knock.
Who's there?
Juanita.
Juanita who?
Juanita lunch with me?

Knock-knock.
Who's there?
June.
June who?
June know by now if you let me in!

Knock-knock.
Who's there?
Kala.
Kala who?
Kala the kettle black!

Knock-knock.
Who's there?
Karen.
Karen who?
Karen a torch for you!

Knock-knock.
Who's there?
Katherine.
Katherine who?
Katherine a speeding bullet!

Knock-knock.
Who's there?
Keshia.
Keshia who?
Keshia if you open the door!

Knock-knock.
Who's there?
Kimmy.
Kimmy who?
Kimmy a kiss!

Knock-knock.
Who's there?
Lacey.
Lacey who?
Lacey days of summer!

Knock-knock.
Who's there?
Lakme.
Lakme who?
Lakme, Stefanie joined the swimming team.

Knock-knock.
Who's there?
Lana.
Lana who?
Lana plenty!

Knock-knock.
Who's there?
Leah.
Leah who?
Leah egg!

Knock-knock.
Who's there?
Lily.
Lily who?
Lily liver!

Knock-knock.
Who's there?
Lisa.
Lisa who?
Lisa on life!

Knock-knock.
Who's there?
Leonie.
Leonie who?
Leonie one you love!

Knock-knock.
Who's there?
Liz.
Liz who?
Lizen to me, I have done this before.

Knock-knock.
Who's there?
Lucy.
Lucy who?
Lucy cannon!

Knock-knock.
Who's there?
Mamie.
Mamie who?
Mamie a cake as fast as you can!

Knock-knock.
Who's there?
Mandy.
Mandy who?
Mandy battle stations!

Knock-knock.
Who's there?
Margo.
Margo who?
Margo, I have work to do.

Knock-knock.
Who's there?
Mary.
Mary who?
Beats me.

Knock-knock.
Who's there?
Maude.
Maude who?
Maude-ern times!

Knock-knock.
Who's there?
Mavis.
Mavis who?
Mavis be the happiest day of your life!

Knock-knock.
Who's there?
Meg.
Meg who?
Meg hay while the sun shines!

Knock-knock.
Who's there?
Michelle.
Michelle who?
Michelle if you want to be heard.

Knock-knock.
Who's there?
Mimi.
Mimi who?
Mimi halfway!

Knock-knock.
Who's there?
Minnie.
Minnie who?
Minnie people laugh at my knock-knock jokes!

Knock-knock.
Who's there?
Nadia.
Nadia who?
Nadia head if you agree with me.

Knock-knock.
Who's there?
Neva.
Neva who?
Neva keep me waiting!

Knock-knock.
Who's there?
Olive.
Olive who?
Olive to please!

Knock-knock.
Who's there?
Ona.
Ona who?
Ona your own home!

Knock-knock.
Who's there?
Patty.
Patty who?
Patty wagon!

Knock-knock.
Who's there?
Polly.
Polly who?
Polly my leg!

Knock-knock.
Who's there?
Rita.
Rita who?
Rita book!

Knock-knock.
Who's there?
Rhonda.
Rhonda who?
Rhonda corner!

Knock-knock.
Who's there?
Sandy.
Sandy who?
Sandy wood before you stain it.

Knock-knock.
Who's there?
Sigrid.
Sigrid who?
Sigrid Service!

Knock-knock.
Who's there?
Stella.
Stella who?
Stella hour until lunch!

Knock-knock.
Who's there?
Trudy.
Trudy who?
Trudy your school!

Knock-knock.
Who's there?
Phyllis.
Phyllis who?
Phyllis buster!

Knock-knock.
Who's there?
Tilly.
Tilly who?
Tilly cows come home!

Ben and Anna Split—Teams

Knock-knock.
Who's there?
Al and Eda.
Al and Eda who?
Al and Eda love, love, Al and Eda love!

Knock-knock.
Who's there?
Alva and Alma.
Alva and Alma who?
Alva day long Alma waiting for you to answer the door!

Knock-knock.
Who's there?
Anatol and Hugh.
Anatol and Hugh who?
Anatol Hugh already who I am!

Knock-knock.
Who's there?
Asta and Atilla.
Asta and Atilla who?
Asta me no questions and Atilla you no lies!

Knock-knock.
Who's there?
Ben and Anna.
Ben and Anna who?
Ben and Anna split!

Knock-knock.
Who's there?
Cain and Abel.
Cain and Abel who?
Cain play today—Abel tomorrow!

Knock-knock.
Who's there?
Butch and Jimmie.
Butch and Jimmie who?
Butch your arms around me and Jimmie a kiss!

Knock-knock.
Who's there?
Jess and Levy.
Jess and Levy who?
Jess go away and Levy me alone!

Knock-knock.
Who's there?
Ken and Wayne.
Ken and Wayne who?
Ken I come in and wait for the Wayne to stop?

Knock-knock.
Who's there?
Lettuce and Will.
Lettuce and Will who?
Lettuce in and Will stop bothering you!

Knock-knock.
Who's there?
Luke and Yul.
Luke and Yul who?
Luke through the keyhole and Yul see!

Knock-knock.
Who's there?
Megan and Chick.
Megan and Chick who?
Megan a list and Chick'in' it twice!

Knock-knock.
Who's there?
Maia and Yvette.
Maia and Yvette who?
Maia cat was sick and Yvette made her better!

Knock-knock.
Who's there?
Olga and Greta.
Olga and Greta who?
Olga home and Greta my keys!

Knock-knock.
Who's there?
Seiko and Geisha.
Seiko and Geisha who?
Seiko and Geishall find!

Knock-knock.
Who's there?
Sid and Shad.
Sid and Shad who?
Sid down and Shad up!

Knock-knock.
Who's there?
Woody and Les.
Woody and Les who?
Woody you open the door and Les me in!

Knock-knock.
Who's there?
Effie and Ida.
Effie and Ida who?
Effie'd known you were coming, Ida baked a cake!

Knock-knock.
Who's there?
Hope and Hugh.
Hope and Hugh who?
Hopen the door and Hugh'll see!

63

Knock-knock.
Who's there?
Jimmie and Hy.
Jimmie and Hy who?
Jimmie a dollar and Hy'll pay you back!

Knock-knock.
Who's there?
Paul and Greta.
Paul and Greta who?
Paul cat's tail and you'll Greta scratch!

Knock-knock.
Who's there?
Stan and Della.
Stan and Della who?
Stand and Della-iver!

Knock-knock.
Who's there?
Bea and Len.
Bea and Len who?
Bea friend and Len me some money!

Knock-knock.
Who's there?
Abbott and Costello.
Abbott and Costello who?
Abbott the Knicks would win the game and now it'll Costello
a lot of money!

Knock-knock.
Who's there?
Ada and Ina.
Ada and Ina who?
Ada big dinner and Ina got sick!

Knock-knock.
Who's there?
Adam and Eve.
Adam and Eve who?
Adam broke and Even the lake was flooded!

Knock-knock.
Who's there?
Agate and Obsidian.
Agate and Obsidian who?
Agate your message and Obsidian here waiting for you!

Knock-knock.
Who's there?
Hugh and Alcott.
Hugh and Alcott who?
Hugh pour the tea and Alcott the cake!

Knock-knock.
Who's there?
Ike and Ali.
Ike and Ali who?
Ike kept knocking and Ali time you knew it was me!

Knock-knock.
Who's there?
Kermit and Althea.
Kermit and Althea who?
Kermit a crime and Althea in jail!

Knock-knock.
Who's there?
Largo and Andante.
Largo and Andante who?
Largo visit my uncle and Andante!

Knock-knock.
Who's there?
Annie and Evie.
Annie and Evie who?
Annie-body and Evie-body!

Knock-knock.
Who's there?
Avis and Hertz.
Avis and Hertz who?
Avis stung by a bee and it Hertz!

Knock-knock.
Who's there?
Beth and Connie.
Beth and Connie who?
Beth wishes and Connie-gratulations!

Knock-knock.
Who's there?
Betty and Lou.
Betty and Lou who?
Betty Lou all your money at the track.

Knock-knock.
Who's there?
Brook and Lynn.
Brook and Lynn who?
Brooklyn, New York, of course!

Knock-knock.
Who's there?
Carmen and Cohen.
Carmen and Cohen who?
Carmen on Friday and Cohen on Sunday!

Knock-knock.
Who's there?
Carrie and Clay.
Carrie and Clay who?
Carrie me home and Clay me down, I'm tired!

Knock-knock.
Who's there?
Meg and Cher.
Meg and Cher who?
Meg some cookies and Cher them with me!

Knock-knock.
Who's there?
Keith and Cosmo.
Keith and Cosmo who?
Keith on complaining and you'll Cosmo trouble!

Knock-knock.
Who's there?
Danielle and Butch.
Danielle and Butch who?
Danielle at me and Butch a smile on your face!

Knock-knock.
Who's there?
Eileen and Ringo.
Eileen and Ringo who?
Eileen against the door and Ringo the bell.

Knock-knock.
Who's there?
Fergie and Liza.
Fergie and Liza who?
Fergie Liza the lawn tomorrow.

Knock-knock.
Who's there?
Ike and Tilly.
Ike and Tilly who?
Ike and Tilly phone you later.

Knock-knock.
Who's there?
Lucy and Desi.
Lucy and Desi who?
Lucy you belt and Desi a reason why your pants fall down.

Knock-knock.
Who's there?
Jimmie and Don.
Jimmie and Don who?
Jimmie my money and Don mess around!

Knock-knock.
Who's there?
Dutch and Hugh.
Dutch and Hugh who?
Dutch me and Hugh'll be sorry!

Knock-knock.
Who's there?
Esau and Evan.
Esau and Evan who?
Esau a ghost and Evan't been the same since!

Knock-knock.
Who's there?
Eyes and Ears.
Eyes and Ears who?
Eyes got another knock-knock joke and Ears it is!

Knock-knock.
Who's there?
Fedora and Derby.
Fedora and Derby who?
Fedora's shut and Derby no one home!

Knock-knock.
Who's there?
Jung and Freud.
Jung and Freud who?
Jung as a puppy and Freud of his own shadow!

Knock-knock.
Who's there?
Isa and Alma.
Isa and Alma who?
Isa you and Alma in love!

Knock-knock.
Who's there?
Gunnar and Flo.
Gunnar and Flo who?
Gunnar huff and puff and Flo your house down!

Knock-knock.
Who's there?
Halibut and Lemming.
Halibut and Lemming who?
Halibut opening this door and Lemming me in!

Knock-knock.
Who's there?
Hobbit and Pixie.
Hobbit and Pixie who?
Hobbit letting me in and Pixie me some lunch!

Knock-knock.
Who's there?
Ida and Bernie.
Ida and Bernie who?
Ida Bernie the toast.

Knock-knock.
Who's there?
Igor and Ira.
Igor and Ira who?
Igor away and Ira-turn!

Knock-knock.
Who's there?
O'Keefe and Hugh.
O'Keefe and Hugh who?
O'Keefe me one more chance and Hugh won't regret it!

Knock-knock.
Who's there?
Lucinda and Les.
Lucinda and Les who?
Lucinda chain and Les me in!

Knock-knock.
Who's there?
Meg and Lyle.
Meg and Lyle who?
Meg that shot and Lyle be a monkey's uncle!

Knock-knock.
Who's there?
Lewis and Maude.
Lewis and Maude who?
Lewis all your money and Maude as well go home!

Knock-knock.
Who's there?
Rhoda and Will.
Rhoda and Will who?
Rhoda boat and Will get there faster!

Knock-knock.
Who's there?
Nanny and Ida.
Nanny and Ida who?
Nanny my friends have any money and Ida either!

Knock-knock.
Who's there?
Noble and Peer.
Noble and Peer who?
Noble, so I knocked, and Peer you are!

Knock-knock.
Who's there?
Omega or Alpha.
Omega or Alpha who?
Omega your mind or Alpha go away!

Knock-knock.
Who's there?
Oz and Toto.
Oz and Toto who?
Oz cold and Totolly frozen!

Knock-knock.
Who's there?
Canon and Rector.
Canon and Rector who?
Canon drive and Rector the car!

Knock-knock.
Who's there?
Evan and Ethan.
Evan and Ethan who?
Evan a picnic and Ethan lunch!

Knock-knock.
Who's there?
Ima and Howie.
Ima and Howie who?
Ima fine and Howie you?

Knock-knock.
Who's there?
Meg and Ada.
Meg and Ada who?
Meg a cake and Ada the whole thing!

Knock-knock.
Who's there?
Pat and Lenny.
Pat and Lenny who?
Pat and Lenny shoes.

Knock-knock.
Who's there?
Renata and Milt.
Renata and Milt who?
Renata Milt during the party.

Knock-knock.
Who's there?
Scum and Deluxe.
Scum and Deluxe who?
Scum to Scotland and see Deluxe Ness Monster!

Knock-knock.
Who's there?
Ike, Isa, and Icon.
Ike, Isa, and Icon who?
I came, I saw, I conquered!

Knock-knock.
Who's there?
Audrey and Rose.
Audrey and Rose who?
Audrey Rose early in the morning.

Knock-knock.
Who's there?
Stan and Bee.
Stan and Bee who?
Stan and Bee counted.

Knock-knock.
Who's there?
Mike and Angel.
Mike and Angel who?
Mike and Angelo.

Knock-knock.
Who's there?
Willie and Nell.
Willie and Nell who?
Willie Nell if we come home late?

Knock-knock.
Who's there?
Jim and Tom.
Jim and Tom who?
Jim and Tomic.

Knock-knock.
Who's there?
Frank and Bea.
Frank and Bea who?
Frank and Beans.

Knock-knock.
Who's there?
Leek and Hal.
Leek and Hal who?
Leek Hal weapon.

Knock-knock.
Who's there?
Sam and Cher.
Sam and Cher who?
"Sam Cher over the Rainbow, way up high . . ."

Knock-knock.
Who's there?
Hook and Dial.
Hook and Dial who?
Hook and Dial Dundee.

Knock-knock.
Who's there?
Ali and Barbara.
Ali and Barbara who?
Ali Barbara and the forty thieves.

Knock-knock.
Who's there?
Pappy and Bertha.
Pappy and Bertha who?
Pappy Berthaday.

Knock-knock.
Who's there?
Leslie and Lee.
Leslie and Lee who?
Leslie the party and Bea alone.

Knock-knock.
Who's there?
Muffin and Toby.
Muffin and Toby who?
Muffin to do but Toby lazy.

Knock-knock.
Who's there?
Dude and Ron.
Dude and Ron who?
Duderonomy.

Knock-knock.
Who's there?
Emily and Grace.
Emily and Grace who?
Emily Grace me, my sweet embraceable you.

Kermit a Crime and You'll Get Caught— TV Shows

The Brady Bunch

Knock-knock.
Who's there?
Mike.
Mike who?
Mike makes right!

Knock-knock.
Who's there?
Carol.
Carol who?
Carol send a package to Africa!

Knock-knock.
Who's there?
Alice.
Alice who?
Alice well!

Knock-knock.
Who's there?
Greg.
Greg who?
Gregs on toast!

Knock-knock.
Who's there?
Marcia.
Marcia who?
Marcia yourself down to the principal's office!

Knock-knock.
Who's there?
Peter.
Peter who?
Peter butter!

Knock-knock.
Who's there?
Jan.
Jan who?
Jan't you let me in?

Knock-knock.
Who's there?
Bobby.
Bobby who?
Bobby pin!

Knock-knock.
Who's there?
Cindy.
Cindy who?
Cindy letter by mail!

The Partridge Family

Knock-knock.
Who's there?
Shirley.
Shirley who?
Shirley you recognize me!

Knock-knock.
Who's there?
Keith.
Keith who?
Keith don't work, that's why I'm knocking!

Knock-knock.
Who's there?
Laurie.
Laurie who?
Laurie your voice, you're shouting!

Knock-knock.
Who's there?
Danny.
Danny who?
Danny the torpedoes, full speed ahead!

Knock-knock.
Who's there?
Chris.
Chris who?
Christmas carol!

Knock-knock.
Who's there?
Tracy.
Tracy who?
Tracy paper!

Knock-knock.
Who's there?
Reuben.
Reuben who?
Reuben salt in my wounds!

Bewitched

Knock-knock.
Who's there?
Samantha.
Samantha who?
Samantha with you?

Knock-knock.
Who's there?
Darrin.
Darrin who?
Darrin the lead!

Knock-knock.
Who's there?
Endora.
Endora who?
Endora games aren't as much fun as outdoor games!

86

Knock-knock.
Who's there?
Tabitha.
Tabitha who?
Tabitha hard things to break!

Knock-knock.
Who's there?
Serena.
Serena who?
Serena 'round the bathtub!

Knock-knock.
Who's there?
Louise.
Louise who?
Louise short for Lewis!

Knock-knock.
Who's there?
Gladys.
Gladys who?
Gladys my last knock-knock joke?

Knock-knock.
Who's there?
Abner.
Abner who?
Abner you, my dear Alfonse!

Knock-knock.
Who's there?
Arthur.
Arthur who?
Arthur any funnier knock-knock jokes?

Knock-knock.
Who's there?
Clara.
Clara who?
Clara the decks!

The Beverly Hillbillies

Knock-knock.
Who's there?
Jed.
Jed who?
Jed'ver hear such funny knock-knock jokes?

Knock-knock.
Who's there?
Granny.
Granny who?
Granny me a wish!

Knock-knock.
Who's there?
Jethro.
Jethro who?
Jethro the boat!

Knock-knock.
Who's there?
Elly May.
Elly May who?
Elly Mayntary, my dear Watson!

Knock-knock.
Who's there?
Miss Jane.
Miss Jane who?
Miss Jane'ken identity!

Green Acres

Knock-knock.
Who's there?
Oliver.
Oliver who?
Oliver you alone if you open the door!

Knock-knock.
Who's there?
Lisa.
Lisa who?
Lisa you can do is open the door!

Knock-knock.
Who's there?
Arnold.
Arnold who?
Arnold you going to let me in?

Knock-knock.
Who's there?
Haney.
Haney who?
Haney days and Sundays always get me down!

Knock-knock.
Who's there?
Ziffel.
Ziffel who?
Ziffel ball!

The Cosby Show

Knock-knock.
Who's there?
Cliff.
Cliff who?
Cliff your fingernails, they're too long!

Knock-knock.
Who's there?
Clair.
Clair who?
Clair sailing!

Knock-knock.
Who's there?
Denise.
Denise who?
Denise is the daughter of the uncle!

Knock-knock.
Who's there?
Theo.
Theo who?
Theo'ld mill stream!

Knock-knock.
Who's there?
Vanessa.
Vanessa who?
Vanessa time I won't ask so nicely!

Knock-knock.
Who's there?
Rudy.
Rudy who?
Rudy toot toot!

Knock-knock.
Who's there?
Olivia.
Olivia who?
Olivia the life of Riley!

Knock-knock.
Who's there?
Sondra.
Sondra who?
Sondra tip of my tongue!

Knock-knock.
Who's there?
Winnie.
Winnie who?
Winnie the Pooh!

Knock-knock.
Who's there?
Nelson.
Nelson who?
Nelson hammers will build a house!

Knock-knock.
Who's there?
Pam.
Pam who?
Pam and eggs!

The Golden Girls

Knock-knock.
Who's there?
Dorothy.
Dorothy who?
Dorothynk I'm stupid, but I can't remember my name!

Knock-knock.
Who's there?
Blanche.
Blanche who?
Blanche not!

Knock-knock.
Who's there?
Rose.
Rose who?
Rose and rows of new cars!

Knock-knock.
Who's there?
Sophia.
Sophia who?
Sophia that way, if you don't remember me!

Designing Women

Knock-knock.
Who's there?
Julia.
Julia who?
Julia love me?

Knock-knock.
Who's there?
Mary Jo.
Mary Jo who?
Mary Jo'll end in divorce!

Knock-knock.
Who's there?
Suzanne.
Suzanne who?
Suzanne socks!

Knock-knock.
Who's there?
Anthony.
Anthony who?
Anthony the door is very polite!

Knock-knock.
Who's there?
Charlene.
Charlene who?
Charlene to meet you, my dear!

Knock-knock.
Who's there?
Carlene.
Carlene who?
Carlene iron!

Sesame Street

Knock-knock.
Who's there?
Ernie.
Ernie who?
Ernie a living!

Knock-knock.
Who's there?
Bert.
Bert who?
Bert in the hand is worth two in the bush!

Knock-knock.
Who's there?
Grover.
Grover who?
Grover to the store and buy some milk!

Knock-knock.
Who's there?
Oscar.
Oscar who?
Oscar foolish question, get a foolish answer!

Knock-knock.
Who's there?
Kermit.
Kermit who?
Kermit a crime and you'll get caught!

Murphy Brown

Knock-knock.
Who's there?
Murphy.
Murphy who?
Murphy sakes alive!

Knock-knock.
Who's there?
Eldin.
Eldin who?
Eldin to your hat, it's windy!

Knock-knock.
Who's there?
Jim.
Jim who?
Jim dandy!

Knock-knock.
Who's there?
Corky.
Corky who?
Corky the bottle!

Knock-knock.
Who's there?
Miles.
Miles who?
Miles when you say that, stranger!

Knock-knock.
Who's there?
Phil.
Phil who?
Phil up the gas tank, and let's go for a ride!

Vampire State Building— Things, etc.

Knock-knock.
Who's there?
Amagansett.
Amagansett who?
Amagansett all.

Knock-knock.
Who's there?
Armageddon.
Armageddon who?
Armageddon a new car!

Knock-knock.
Who's there?
Avenue.
Avenue who?
Avenue learned my name yet?

Knock-knock.
Who's there?
Atlas.
Atlas who?
Atlas report, the Mets were winning!

Knock-knock.
Who's there?
Baghdad.
Baghdad who?
Baghdad turkey.

Knock-knock.
Who's there?
Bashful.
Bashful who?
Bashful of corn!

Knock-knock.
Who's there?
Basket.
Basket who?
Basket-Robbins!

Knock-knock.
Who's there?
Big Dipper.
Big Dipper who?
I Big to Dipper with you.

Knock-knock.
Who's there?
Bull.
Bull who?
Bull the chain.

Knock-knock.
Who's there?
Bush.
Bush who?
Bush the door.

Knock-knock.
Who's there?
Canoe.
Canoe who?
Canoe lend me a dollar?

Knock-knock.
Who's there?
Card.
Card who?
Card to please!

Knock-knock.
Who's there?
Cargo.
Cargo who?
Cargo fast in fourth gear!

Knock-knock.
Who's there?
Census.
Census who?
Census part of dollars!

Knock-knock.
Who's there?
Chrome.
Chrome who?
Chromosome.

Knock-knock.
Who's there?
Dachshund.
Dachshund who?
The ship will dachshund.

Knock-knock.
Who's there?
Denial.
Denial who?
Denial is a river in Egypt!

Knock-knock.
Who's there?
Derby.
Derby who?
Derby dozen.

Knock-knock.
Who's there?
Diesel.
Diesel who?
Diesel be the best jokes you ever heard!

Knock-knock.
Who's there?
Diploma.
Diploma who?
Diploma to fix the pipes!

Knock-knock.
Who's there?
Disc.
Disc who?
Disc is my best knock-knock joke!

Knock-knock.
Who's there?
Dish.
Dish who?
Dish is silly!

Knock-knock.
Who's there?
Donatello.
Donatello who?
Donatello lie!

Knock-knock.
Who's there?
Dopey.
Dopey who?
Dopey stupid.

Knock-knock.
Who's there?
Dozen.
Dozen who?
Dozen anybody know my name?

Knock-knock.
Who's there?
Ellery Queen.
Ellery Queen who?
Ellery Queen her room tomorrow.

Knock-knock.
Who's there?
Exorcist.
Exorcist who?
To exorcist regularly is important!

Knock-knock.
Who's there?
Expensive.
Expensive who?
Expensive for hire.

Knock-knock.
Who's there?
Fella.
Fella who?
Fella the leader!

Knock-knock.
Who's there?
Frankenstein.
Frankenstein who?
Frankenstein the contract whenever he's ready.

Knock-knock.
Who's there?
Gandhi.
Gandhi who?
Gandhi ropes!

Knock-knock.
Who's there?
Golden Gate.
Golden Gate who?
Golden Gate me a glass of water, please.

Knock-knock.
Who's there?
Gnu.
Gnu who?
Gnu brooms sweep clean!

Knock-knock.
Who's there?
Gorilla.
Gorilla who?
Gorilla me a steak!

Knock-knock.
Who's there?
Gutter.
Gutter who?
Gutter some flowers and she'll forgive you!

Knock-knock.
Who's there?
Handsome.
Handsome who?
Handsome dishes to your father, please.

Knock-knock.
Who's there?
Harmony.
Harmony who?
Harmony roads must a man walk down before you can call him a man?

Knock-knock.
Who's there?
Haydn.
Haydn who?
Haydn out.

Knock-knock.
Who's there?
Heifer.
Heifer who?
Heifer seen a ghost?

Knock-knock.
Who's there?
Herd.
Herd who?
Herd my hand knocking on this door!

Knock-knock.
Who's there?
Hose.
Hose who?
Hose been sleeping in my bed?

Knock-knock.
Who's there?
Howl.
Howl who?
Howl in the world are you doin'?

Knock-knock.
Who's there?
Iguana.
Iguana who?
Iguana rule the world!

Knock-knock.
Who's there?
Iowa.
Iowa who?
Iowa a lot of money.

Knock-knock.
Who's there?
Irene Dunne.
Irene Dunne who?
Irene Dunne a lot today.

Knock-knock.
Who's there?
Ivory.
Ivory who?
Ivory about you!

Knock-knock.
Who's there?
Jester.
Jester who?
Jester old-fashioned girl!

Knock-knock.
Who's there?
Julie Andrews.
Julie Andrews who?
Julie Andrews a pretty picture.

Knock-knock.
Who's there?
Kipper.
Kipper who?
Kipper Gore!

Knock-knock.
Who's there?
Kismet.
Kismet who?
Kismet once, and kiss me twice, and kiss me once again . . .

Knock-knock.
Who's there?
Knees.
Knees who?
Knees-ter Bunny!

Knock-knock.
Who's there?
Lasso.
Lasso who?
Lasso someone and make a million bucks!

Knock-knock.
Who's there?
Leaf.
Leaf who?
Leaf me be!

Knock-knock.
Who's there?
Lock.
Lock who?
Lock for the silver lining!

Knock-knock.
Who's there?
Madonna.
Madonna who?
Madonna give me trouble.

Knock-knock.
Who's there?
Malta.
Malta who?
Malta milk.

Knock-knock.
Who's there?
Manchu.
Manchu who?
Manchu a lot.

Knock-knock.
Who's there?
Moses.
Moses who?
Moses the lawn, it needs it.

Knock-knock.
Who's there?
Mountain.
Mountain who?
Mountain debts.

Knock-knock.
Who's there?
Musket.
Musket who?
Musket a doorbell, I've been knocking forever!

Knock-knock.
Who's there?
Mustard.
Mustard who?
Mustard left it at home.

Knock-knock.
Who's there?
Nanny.
Nanny who?
Nanny your beeswax!

Knock-knock.
Who's there?
Ninja.
Ninja who?
Ninja just have a candy bar?

Knock-knock.
Who's there?
Nike.
Nike who?
Nike night.

Knock-knock.
Who's there?
Nobody.
Nobody who?
Nobody, get it.

Knock-knock.
Who's there?
Oil.
Oil who?
Oil be seeing you!

Knock-knock.
Who's there?
Paris.
Paris who?
Paris the broccoli, please.

Knock-knock.
Who's there?
Pasta.
Pasta who?
Pasta salt, please.

Knock-knock.
Who's there?
Pecan.
Pecan who?
Pecan boo.

Knock-knock.
Who's there?
Perrot.
Perrot who?
Perrot away the garbage.

Knock-knock.
Who's there?
Phone.
Phone who?
Phonely I had known!

Knock-knock.
Who's there?
Pencil.
Pencil who?
Pencil fall down if you don't wear suspenders!

Knock-knock.
Who's there?
Pill.
Pill who?
Pillowcase!

Knock-knock.
Who's there?
Pitcher.
Pitcher who?
Pitcher right foot in, pitcher right foot out, and you do the hokeypokey and you shake yourself about!

Knock-knock.
Who's there?
Pits.
Pits who?
Pit's only a paper moon!

Knock-knock.
Who's there?
Pizza.
Pizza who?
Pizza this, piece of that.

Knock-knock.
Who's there?
Police.
Police who?
Police come out and play!

Knock-knock.
Who's there?
Radial.
Radial who?
Radial free Europe.

Knock-knock.
Who's there?
Razor.
Razor who?
Razor hand if you have a question!

Knock-knock.
Who's there?
Rio.
Rio who?
Riorrange your room.

Knock-knock.
Who's there?
Rodin.
Rodin who?
Rodin the window, please.

Knock-knock.
Who's there?
Santa Cruz.
Santa Cruz who?
Santa Cruz through the sky.

Knock-knock.
Who's there?
Scold.
Scold who?
Scold at the North Pole.

Knock-knock.
Who's there?
Sheik.
Sheik who?
Sheik-speare!

Knock-knock.
Who's there?
Siena.
Siena who?
Siena thing good?

Knock-knock.
Who's there?
Sneezie.
Sneezie who?
Sneezie kind of guy.

Knock-knock.
Who's there?
Snow.
Snow who?
Snow business like show business!

Knock-knock.
Who's there?
Sofa.
Sofa who?
Sofa, so good!

Knock-knock.
Who's there?
Speck.
Speck who?
Speck softly and carry a big stick!

Knock-knock.
Who's there?
Sprocket.
Sprocket who?
Sprocketti!

Knock-knock.
Who's there?
Stapler.
Stapler who?
Stapler stocks are the best investment!

Knock-knock.
Who's there?
Summer.
Summer who?
Summer good, some are bad.

Knock-knock.
Who's there?
Sundance.
Sundance who?
Sundance, some don't.

Knock-knock.
Who's there?
Sunkist.
Sunkist who?
Sunkist, some hugged.

Knock-knock.
Who's there?
Tango.
Tango who?
Tango away in the winter.

Knock-knock.
Who's there?
Tennis.
Tennis who?
Tennis twice five!

Knock-knock.
Who's there?
Thermos.
Thermos who?
Thermos be a better way!

Knock-knock.
Who's there?
Thistle.
Thistle who?
Thistle be my last knock-knock joke!

Knock-knock.
Who's there?
Thighs.
Thighs who?
Thighs the limit!

Knock-knock.
Who's there?
Thumb.
Thumb who?
Thumb day my prince will come!

Knock-knock.
Who's there?
Toupee.
Toupee who?
Toupee is the first day of the rest of your life!

Knock-knock.
Who's there?
Tooth.
Tooth who?
Tooth or Consequences!

Knock-knock.
Who's there?
Toto.
Toto who?
Toto recall.

Knock-knock.
Who's there?
Truman.
Truman who?
Truman are hard to find.

Knock-knock.
Who's there?
Tuba.
Tuba who?
Tuba toothpaste!

Knock-knock.
Who's there?
Vampire.
Vampire who?
Vampire State Building!

Knock-knock.
Who's there?
Vaults.
Vaults who?
Vaults-ing Matilda!

Knock-knock.
Who's there?
Voodoo.
Voodoo who?
Voodoo you think you're foolin'?

Knock-knock.
Who's there?
Wallet.
Wallet who?
Wallet you play with us today!

Knock-knock.
Who's there?
Weasel.
Weasel who?
Weasel, you buy.

Knock-knock.
Who's there?
Weevil.
Weevil who?
Weevil overcome!

Knock-knock.
Who's there?
Yacht.
Yacht who?
Yacht to get a doorbell!

Knock-knock.
Who's there?
Yeast.
Yeast who?
It's the yeast you can do.

Knock-knock.
Who's there?
Yoga.
Yoga who?
Yoga too far!

Knock-knock.
Who's there?
Yorkie.
Yorkie who?
Yorkie doesn't work.

Knock-knock.
Who's there?
Zephyr.
Zephyr who?
Zephyr the police, there's a prowler outside!

About the Author

Dora Wood lives in New York City. She has also written *500 Wacky Knock-Knock Jokes for Kids*, *500 Hilarious Knock-Knock Jokes for Kids*, and *500 More Wild and Wacky Knock-Knock Jokes for Kids*.

Knock-knock.
Who's there?
Summer.
Summer who?
Summer good, some are bad,
but all of these jokes are guaranteed fun!

Published by Ballantine Books.

Call toll free 1-800-793-BOOK (2665) to order by phone and use your major credit card. Or use this coupon to order by mail.

__500 HILARIOUS KNOCK-KNOCK JOKES FOR KIDS	345-38160-2	$3.99
__500 MORE WILD AND WACKY KNOCK-KNOCK JOKES FOR KIDS	345-38161-0	$3.99
__500 WACKY KNOCK-KNOCK JOKES FOR KIDS	345-38080-0	$3.99
__500 WILD KNOCK-KNOCK JOKES FOR KIDS	345-38159-9	$4.00
__1001 DINOSAUR JOKES FOR KIDS	345-38498-2	$3.99
__OH NO! NOT ANOTHER 1,000 JOKES FOR KIDS	345-34035-3	$4.99
__1,000 CRAZY JOKES FOR KIDS	345-34694-7	$4.99
__1,000 JOKES FOR KIDS OF ALL AGES	345-33480-9	$4.99
__1,000 KNOCK KNOCK JOKES FOR KIDS	345-33481-7	$4.99
__1,000 MORE JOKES FOR KIDS	345-34034-5	$4.00
__1,000 HOWLERS FOR KIDS	345-36155-5	$4.99
__1,000 MONSTER JOKES FOR KIDS	345-35895-3	$4.99
__1,000 WHAT'S WHAT JOKES FOR KIDS	345-34654-8	$4.99

Name_____
Address_____
City_____State_____Zip_____

Please send me the BALLANTINE BOOKS I have checked above.
I am enclosing $_____
  plus
Postage & handling* $_____
Sales tax (where applicable) $_____
Total amount enclosed $_____

*Add $4 for the first book and $1 for each additional book.

Send check or money order (no cash or CODs) to:
Ballantine Mail Sales, 400 Hahn Road, Westminster, MD 21157.

Prices and numbers subject to change without notice.
Valid in the U.S. only.
All orders subject to availability.   JOKES